Listen To My Heart

E. GENE GIVENS

COPYRIGHT

Poems copyright © September 2020 and 2026 by e. gene givens.
genegivens@verizon.net

Cover design by e. gene givens.

Spanish translation by e gene givens.

LISTEN TO MY HEART

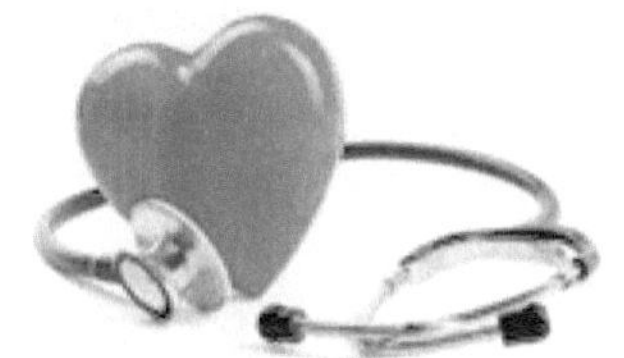

DEDICATION

i attempted to write you a song
using the air as my music
i messed up
and i came out as a poem
that only my heart could sing

CONTENTS

From A Distance

from a distance
i saw you . . .
and as i passed
i marveled at your beauty . . .
a beauty un-compared . . .
a beauty un-remembered

from a distance
our eyes met . . .
and as we passed
you smiled
and poetry of love
un-fulfilled
came to mind

from
a distance
i watched you . . .
you greeted him with a smile . . .
and a kiss
and he responded by whispering
sweet love things in your ear

from a distance
i saw you walk away . . .
and my heart ached
as i stood alone
. . . once more

Like That Old Mason Jar . . .

i was empty
like that old mason jar
in the fruit cellar
i needed an illusion
something comforting
like an old quilted blanket
something warm, soft,
and smooth to the touch
something reassuring
like sunshine after a raging storm
i needed to feel
protected
like a child protects
an ice cream cone
i needed something simple
as simple as a child's imagination
i needed to re-discover *"things"*
with an innocent ear and fresh
eyes
i needed — wanted
to believe that romance
and passion
was still possible
that two people could still care
for one another
and that love was somewhere
out there
patiently waiting . . .
just like that old mason jar
in the fruit cellar

The Truth of the Matter is . . .

i just can't get enough of you
i've tried to convince myself that
you were someone
who was just
passing through
i talk with friends
listening with deaf ears
to their flirtations
as my thoughts rest with
you
i smile
a certain smile
and then they smile too thinking
mine is for them
but this is not true
it's simply because
i just can't get enough of
you

La Verdad De La Materia Es . . .

simplemente no puedo obtener suficiente de
tú
he intentado convencerme
que usted era alguien que estaba de paso
hablo con amigas
escuchando con oídos sordos a
sus coqueteos
como mis pensamientos descansan con
tú
yo sonrío
una cierta sonrisa
y luego sonríen también
pensando que el mío es para ellos
pero esto no es cierto
es simply porque
simplemente no puedo obtener suficiente de
tú

In Search Of . . .

searching . . .
in cincinnati, i was taught to be polite
charming, and considerate to my elders
and people with strange faces
and round bellies

searching . . .
i braved the icy bearing seas
swam the inside passage
and traversed the alaskan musk-kegs
with their hidden sink holes where time
floated and direction was unknown
without a compass or the colored pill
on the 27th day

searching . . .
i patiently suffered the boredom in nashville
the duplicity in new york . . . the lies in d.c.
the doubt in atlanta . . . the pain in san diego
the deceit in portland . . . and the unwarranted
compliments from people in florida, georgia
alabama, and texas
who enjoyed telling me how *"lucky"* i was

searching . . .
i got caught up in the dreams, fantasies,
and expectations of situations
i could not alter, change, or modify

searching . . .
i have visited many lands, gazed upon many
faces found many treasures, and experienced
the many pleasures that only the flesh can offer

it seems that i have done many things
some good – some things less
and undoubtedly
i will do more
in search of love . . .
and unborn babies
that will look like me

If I Could . . .

if i could . . .
i'd speak the words
that would make you understand
see and feel my pain...my regret...
my passion... my need to love,
and to be loved in return
if i could . . . i would

i can tell you anecdotes, stories,
limericks, and rhymes
that may cause you to smile and cry
from time to time
and maybe, now, and then,
if you have the mind
you'll reflect and reminisce about your
own . . . about how cruel and wonderful life
can be
and how much you've grown

but no matter how hard i try
i cannot seem to find the right words,
expression or tone
the right words that will keep me
from being alone . . .

words that would transport you to this
place
a place where i wait to be discovered
this little out of the way place
here i wait for someone to find me . . .
a place where i wait for someone to love
for someone to see, understand
and truly love me
if i could only find the right words . . .

if i could . . . i would

Fascinated By My Skin

fascinated by my skin
you decided to climb in

no – not tonight i mused
i was tired . . .
tired of being used

noticing my distance
you became slow
methodical and persistent
(not used to being refused)

maybe some conversation
a drink and a dance
might lead to romance

so, we danced
you talked
i listened
and took a chance

in the rain we walked, to a breakfast
date even though you kept reminding
me
(and yourself)
that you had to go, it was getting late

to my surprise, you were loud and
rude but that was only a façade
to protect what was sensitive, soft
and smooth

the moment was brief
tender, yet, intense
and i have thought of nothing since . . .
since you became . . .
fascinated with my skin
and decided to climb in

Listen To My Heart

i have shared and possessed
many hearts and souls
at least
that is what i've been told
but no heart that i have
possessed or shared
has compelled me to want
or linger long enough
for us to grow old
i was just looking for a vessel
to store my love in
and then you came
and lent me your heart
i listened when your heart told
me that your love was just
enough to fill my cup
not too much
but just enough . . .
for me

Masterpiece

listening to you speak
i imagined hearing you
on a level higher than
sound . . . your voice faded
and i began
to total your features . . .
how your mouth moved
in perfect harmony
with your hands
as if your arms were
paint brushes
and your fingers
bristles
your mouth
poured out colors . . .
incomprehensible
as your melodic voice
painted a picture of paradise
and when you had finished
your liquid discourse
i had a masterpiece
painted on my soul

A Touch of Tenderness

you fascinate me
and my inner being
you touch me with your
eyes a touch of tenderness
that makes me so aware
of my emptiness
when we are apart
memories run around my
house
like they own it
and your aroma lingers
even after your tenderness
has been washed away

Kansas In July

i dreamt i was the wind
that caressed your thighs
as i cooled you off
on a hot summer's day
as i swirled around you
i danced a dance of love
and my breeze
as it blew through the
trees made them whistle
and sing you my love
songs at days end
as you laid fast asleep . . .
dreaming
i watched you smile
as i tenderly stroked
your delicate body
and hoped . . .
you were dreaming of
me

There Is No Flower

there is no flower
nor thing of beauty that
can compare to you you
are the essence
of all fragrances
a mixture of delusion
and reality
an oasis in space
that all travelers seek
there is no thing
undaunted by your
touch all pain turns to
bliss and when your
nectar overflows
spilling into me
we become as one
and our image is
eternal

Poem For Cesar Bejarano

(to his secret love)

i love you my sweet
this
i admit to myself
though our eyes have refused
to accept it
our hearts will never betray us

someday my sweet
our hearts will unite
just like the bee that
seeks the flower
and the day that seeks
the night

but until then . . .
i will continue to wait
for time . . .
and you

Poema Para Cesar Bejarano

(para su amor secreto)

te quiero me amor
esto
lo admito, a mi, mismo
aunque nuestros ojos han rehusado
aceptarlo
nuestros corazones nunca nos
traicionarán
algún día, mi amor
nuestros corazones se unirán
justo, como la abeja que
busca la flor
y el día que busca
la noche
pero hasta entonces . . .
continuori esperando
por el tiempo . . .
y por ti

Stickers, Slogans, And Logos

before i became a parent
i didn't like to put stickers, slogans
or logos on my car
not on a bumper, window, or dash
i had convinced myself that they
were a distractive eye sore
and felt that they damaged the car's
finish, as well as obscured one's vision
but when i was growing up, it seemed
perfectly all right, even amusing at times . . .

i can remember stealthfully writing
slogans and logos on weathered cars
trucks, and vans, then standing back
with my arms folded, marveling at my art
and naively hoping that the owners
would take my "free" advice. . .

i can still remember sitting in the back seat
steaming up the windows with my breath
fascinated with drawing smiley faces
stick men, and funny animals
i especially liked writing my name backwards
and drawing hearts with my true love's initials
inside **. . .**

and now . . .
i can't help but smile, when my car looks
weathered
and i catch myself scolding my children for
putting stickers on my car, and for writing slogans
and logos all over, or for standing in the back seat,
steaming up the windows to draw smiley faces,
stick men, and funny animals
or when they write their names . . . backwards . . .
in the rear window,
and especially when they start to draw hearts . . .
with their true love's initials inside

In the Rain Forest

there is sanctuary
in the rain forest
under this canopy
where your love
and tranquility abides
here
in this sacred place
one could lose their
heart or mind . . .
or both
waiting . . .
waiting for rainbows
and the peace
between two lovers
to subside

Sinless Lovers

when we were young
and so full of virtue
we gave without asking
and accepted without acknowledgment your
innocent eyes
and the soul of motown
made life so simple . . . so sweet
as we held hands
and each other
as we danced slow and close
under blue lights in steamy basements

when we were young. . .
just being near you
just hearing your soothing voice
was the only answer – nothing else mattered
because you were mine
and i was yours. . . forever
and that was enough

when we were young. . .
everything was so clear – so transparent
there was nothing worth hiding
we just stripped off the flesh
so the bones would show
leaving nothing but two sinless lovers
who were artless and pure
yet, so intense with intent to please
. . . each other

Small Words

there are some waves that crash endlessly
against the rocky shore waiting
for a reseeding tide that will never come
there are some wounds that never heal
they only fester and bleed trying to become a scar
there are some journeys that never end
only to become perpetual wanderings
seeking a place to rest
there are some words that can
fill a space – a void to its highest degree attainable
with depth and intensity
with complexity, strength, and importance
words that can describe the seriousness
of any situation
there are some words that can fill the void
with the depth and breathe that blows
like the wind of a hurricane, or flow like
a soft breeze between the trees
there are some words that can evoke
a vital response to a physical
and emotional experience
or induce some terrible image
of emotional aversion
but there are some words
that are just too small
to convey their real meaning
small words like . . . find . . . or feel . . .
or pain . . . or more . . . or less . . .
high . . . low . . . hate . . . fear . . . or love . . .
love is a little word that is just . . .

too . . . freaking . . . small
to explain what i feel . . .
or when i think about . . .
the essence of you

MÜGE: Lily Of The Valley

from the moment you walked out of my dreams
i wanted to crawl under your skin
and swim in your essence — and not miss a stroke
i wanted to look through those almond shaped eyes
that had hypnotized and captured my soul
i wanted to taste the nectar your tongue had tasted
as it licked, and moistened your sweet, soft, and
supple lips
i wanted to hold you close,
and have you melt in my arms, like butter
on a hot toasted bun
i wanted to make intense love to you
until i was breathless
and as we lay spent from exhaustion
i wanted to watch you drift into sleep
and notice the beads of sweat
          s-l-o-w-l-y
cascade from your skin
forming into small rivers of love
that flowed on forever. . .
but this was only a dream . . .
so, each night i must wait . . . once more
for the glow of the turkish moon
as it shines on the lily of the valley
and wait patiently for your petals to open
so, you will walk out of my dreams. . .
and into my reality

Know This . . .

from the tips of your toes
to the nape of your neck
not one spot on your body
will i miss, or fail to kiss
weariness wears many faces
but there will be no forbidden spaces
no hidden or sacred places
that i will not discover and cover
there will be no secrets to keep
no mysteries to seek
save one – while i'm alive
for where your love resides
my heart and soul seeks to abide for
my love for you
will be faithful, loyal, and true
for this is the least i can promise you
there will be nothing that i can hide
or nothing i will not try
in my search to find
the place where your love hides

Poem xvi: Sunday Afternoon

gray sky . . .
tried to sleep
couldn't
thought I'd get up
and cook
thought again
decide i shouldn't

rain . . .
nothing on tv
john wayne re-runs
and animal shows
just don't do
nothing for me

still raining . . .
you called
we talked
and i emptied
a bottle of wine
unnoticing
ever since that
sunday afternoon
when it rains
i can't think of
anything
but you

Poem xii: Last Night

last night
we made passionate love
and your body was like a generator
producing volts of electricity
currents flowed
through my body
stimulating my mind
making my nerves stand on end
giving birth to my soul

Poem XII: Aroma

the sweet aroma
you left on my sheets
only made me realize
how empty
my life
really is

In Sync

maybe, we were moving too fast
let's slow things down
so we can hear each other's
heart beat
let's stop and listen
to the silence
so we can find the rhythm
let me hold you close and sway
back forth
until our heart beats get in sync
we have the same memories
the same story
so, let me look through your eyes
until i can see things
from your
point of view
let me hold you close
and close my eyes
until i can catch your rhythm
so our love
will be in sync

What I Miss . . .

moon light, stars, and long walks
shared thoughts and quiet talks
to hold her close when we dance
late night and early morning romance
playing cards and games of chance . . .
this is what i miss

no excuses, alibis, or two-faced lies
just simple truth and elegance undisguised
beauty – seen only with my eyes
the smell of flowers bright and sweet
a different scent each time we meet . . .
this is what i miss

long drives to out of the way places candle
lit dinners and fire places
high cheek bones on a perfect face things
soft, like silk and lace
lasting memories that i can't replace . . .
this is what i miss

gazing into her almond eyes
touching and caressing her supple thighs
kisses – long . . . wet . . . and deep
a love that is true . . . forever. . . for keeps . . .
this . . . is what i really miss

Where Have You Gone

where have you gone my love?
my eyes have grown weary searching
and my letters
have gone unanswered
yet
the nightingale still sings

without you
my love
the nights are cold
the days are without time
and the seasons go unchanged

others have come . . . and gone
my love
only their numbers remain . . .
and this emptiness

where have you gone my love?
have you forgotten the promise . . .
the vow we made?
my heart has not
nor the nightingale
his song

I Could Have Loved You Forever

when we were young
loving you was easy
and dreams were there just for the taking
but that was yesterday
and dreams don't always come true
i loved you so much
until it hurt
this i know
because
my heart told me so

i could have spent my whole life loving you
but the future offered uncertain choices
and there seemed to be no safe path for us
so i learned how to hide my feelings
even when i loved you so
and when we looked into tomorrow
fear and doubt were the loudest voices
and only empty choices remained

i didn't want to go
but i just couldn't stay
i could have loved you . . .
forever
because loving you was so easy
but that was yesterday
and i just couldn't stay

Solitaire

love is heaven on earth
that's what they say
but i ain't going to see heaven
unless the good lord
takes
me away my
woman done left me
took the kids and dog too
now this old house is so lonely
can't seem to find
no satisfaction
in nothing i do
even played a game of solitaire
and lost at that too
you know
it's funny
can't even play
a good game of cards
unless there's two

Kool-Aid

sitting
here
missing you
a thought occurred to me
you know
kool-aid
ain't worth a dam . . .
without sugar

Heavy Rain

golden oldies
soulful, slow, and sweet
echo and drift through the air
as memories . . .
memories of yesterday – and you
are stirred up
like dust particles by a gentle wind
spinning, whirling, and twirling
only to settle at my feet . . .
a wish for rain
is my only thought – my only need
rain . . .
clear, fresh, and sweet
heavy rain . . .
heavy enough to wash away these tears
these tears of joy and pain
that flow like rivers
in my memory
from my mind
through my eyes
and down my cheeks
rain. . . heavy rain
clear. . . fresh. . . and sweet

On Cold Mornings

as i wake
reaching/searching
for the warm
and security
that was always you
i find
only
a cold and empty
space
where you
might/should have been
had i not made
your days
like these cold mornings
i wake up to

Under the Cold Winter Moon

turn on your warm light
that shines brightly
under the cold winter moon come heal
these wounds
from eager love
given far too soon
let me rest in your arms
til the dreams become real
and the unwanted pain disappears let
me stay for just a little while and share
the tenderness
of your warm light
that shines so brightly
under this cold winter moon

Bajo La Fría Luna Del Invierno

enciender su luz cálida
que brilla tan brillantemente
bajo la fría luna de invierno
vienen sanar estas heridas
desde de amor ansioso dado demasiado pronto
déjame descansar en tus brazos
hasta que los sueños se vuelvan reales
y el dolor no deseado desaparece
déjame quedarme por sólo un de tiempo
y compartir la ternura
de tu luz cálida
que brilla tan brillantemente
bajo esta fría luna de invierno

Some Journeys May Take Longer. . .

there are times. . .
times when i can remember
how intoxicated i would become
with the sight of you
the tenderness of your touch
and how it made my flesh walk
how i tried to take deep breaths
whenever you were near
trying to drown my senses
with the fragrance of you

and there are times. . .
times when i can taste your very essence
anticipate your every move
think your every thought
mouthing each word before it was spoken

and then there are times. . .
times when your spirit seemed so far away. . .
traveling. . . searching. . . discovering. . .
times when my chest could not find air
and my soul felt lost without you

stubbornly, i admit to myself
that i must learn to be patient. . .
from time to time, everyone must go on
their own "special" journey
perhaps
some journeys are meant to be taken alone
i guess it's true what they say:

> *some journeys may take longer than others*
> *while some will take no time at all*
> *yet, some journeys are never finished*

is this one of those times
one of those "special" kind of journeys?
a journey without notice. . . without direction
a journey without destination. . . without purpose
a journey without. . .
me?

Just A Part . . .

i have always been there for you
i just wanted to help you
find your place in the world
but you just couldn't see...

deep inside
you knew my love was true
i just wished that you had loved me
enough to love me beyond
your doubts... your fears... your regrets

i would risk my life to touch you again
i just wished that you didn't regret
the stolen moments we shared ...
the smiles... the laughter... the bliss

when i think about it...
i know i loved you...
more than life itself
the fact is...
i have always loved you
even though you can't say the same

you were just stuck. . . always looking
at things from/in your past
instead of looking at... seeing
what was right in front of you

and now...
i am just a part of your past ...
a memory...
and you are just a part
of mine